Contents

Aa

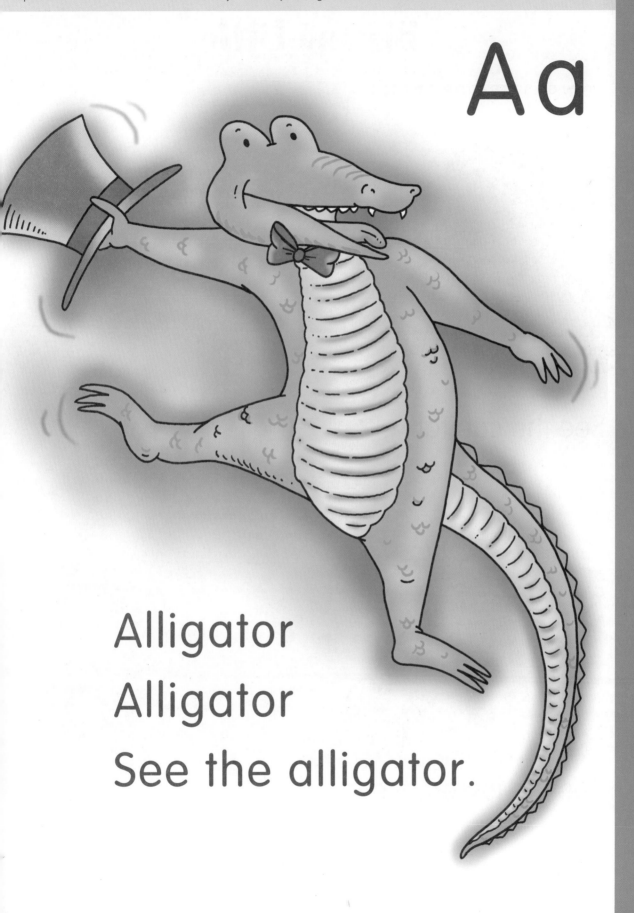

Alligator
Alligator
See the alligator.

Skills:

Matching Upper- and Lowercase Forms of Letters

Using Visual Discrimination

Big and Little

Draw a line to make a match.

See the capital **A**.

See the lowercase **a**.

I Can Write

Trace and write the letters.

A	A	A

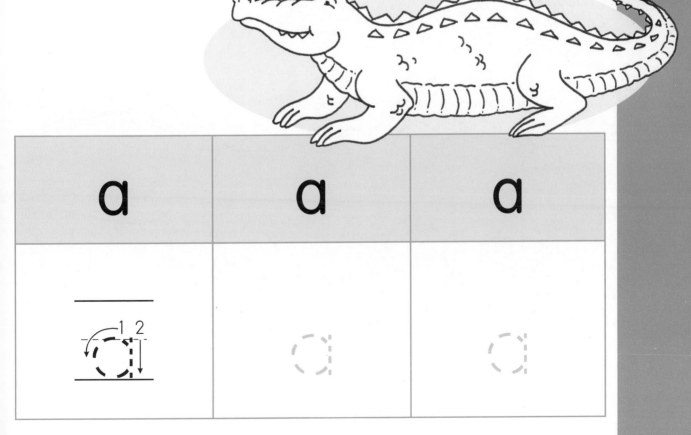

a	a	a

Find It

Circle the letters that are the same as the first letter in each row.

a	a	a	a	b	c
b	b	a	b	c	b
A	A	B	C	A	A

Trace the alligator.
Color it green.

See the alligator.

Fill in the ◯.

1. Find the capital letter.

◯ a

◯ A

2. Find the lowercase letter.

◯ a

◯ A

3. Find the alligator.

 ◯

Give the spelling test. Say:

1. Write a capital A in the box.
2. Write a lowercase a in the box.

Spelling Test

1. ☐

2. ☐

ASSESSMENT 1

B b

Baby

Baby

See the baby.

Note: Throughout the book, read and explain all directions to your child. Provide any needed help to complete the tasks.

Big and Little

Draw a line to make a match.

See the capital **B**.

See the lowercase **b**.

I Can Write

Trace and write the letters.

B	B	B
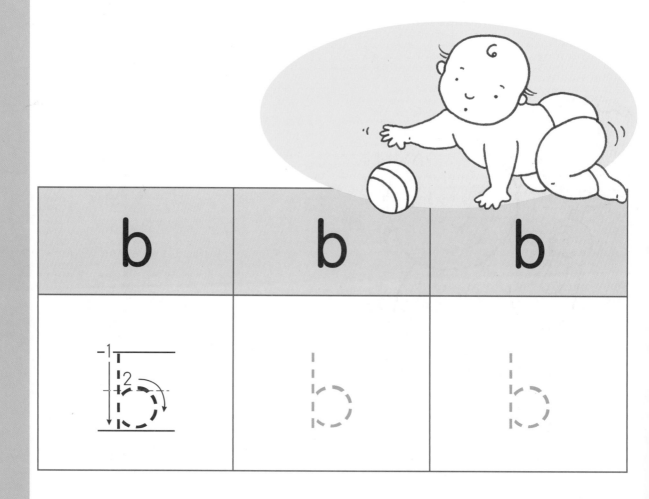	B	B

b	b	b
	b	b

Find It

Circle the letters that are the same as the first letter in each row.

b	b	c	a	b
B	C	A	B	B
a	a	a	b	c

Trace the baby's rattle. Color it red.

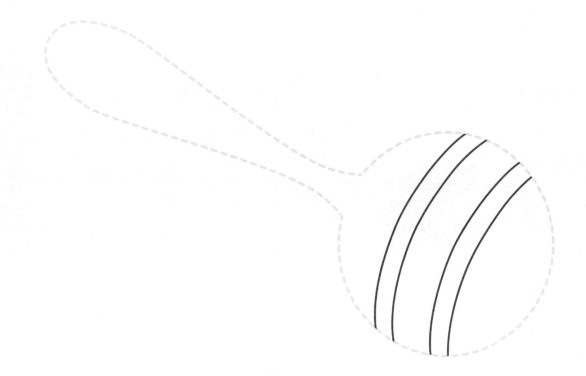

TEST YOUR SKILLS

Fill in the ◯.

1. Find the capital letter.

◯ B

◯ b

2. Find the lowercase letter.

◯ b

◯ B

3. Find the baby.

◯   ◯

Give the spelling test. Say:

1. Write a capital B in the box.
2. Write a lowercase b in the box.

Spelling Test

1. ⬜

2. ⬜

Cc

Cat

Cat

See the cat.

Skills:

Matching Upper- and Lowercase Forms of Letters

Using Visual Discrimination

Big and Little

Draw a line to make a match.

See the capital C.

See the lowercase c.

I Can Write

Trace and write the letters.

C	C	C

C	C	C

Find It

Circle the letters that are the same as the first letter in each row.

C	B	A	C	C
c	a	b	c	c
b	c	b	a	b

Trace the cat.
Color it yellow.

TEST YOUR SKILLS

Fill in the ○.

1. Find the capital letter.

○ C

○ c

2. Find the lowercase letter.

○ c

○ C

3. Find the cat.

○ ○

Give the spelling test. Say:

1. Write a capital C in the box.
2. Write a lowercase C in the box.

Spelling Test

1. ☐

2. ☐

D d

Dinosaur

Dinosaur

See the big dinosaur.

Big and Little

Skills:

Matching
Upper- and
Lowercase
Forms of
Letters

Using Visual
Discrimination

Draw a line to make a match.

See the capital **D**.

See the lowercase **d**.

I Can Write

Trace and write the letters.

D	D	D

d	d	d

Spell & Write • EMC 4535 • © Evan-Moor Corp.

Find It

Circle the letters that are the same as the first letter in each row.

d	D	d	a	d
D	B	C	D	D
c	c	a	b	c

Trace the path to the water.
Color the picture.

Fill in the ◯.

1. Find the capital letter.

◯ D

◯ d

2. Find the lowercase letter.

◯ d

◯ D

3. Find the dinosaur.

◯   ◯

Give the spelling test. Say:
1. Write a capital D in the box.
2. Write a lowercase d in the box.

Spelling Test

1.

2.

Ee

Elephant

Elephant

See the elephant.

Skills:

Matching Upper- and Lowercase Forms of Letters

Using Visual Discrimination

Big and Little

Draw a line to make a match.

See the capital **E**.

See the lowercase **e**.

I Can Write

Trace and write the letters.

E	E	E
	E	E

e e e

Skills:

Identifying
Like Letters

Using Fine
Motor Skills

Find It

Circle the letters that are the same as the first letters in each row.

e	e	E	a	e
B	E	B	A	B
a	b	a	c	a

Trace the path to the peanuts.
Color the picture.

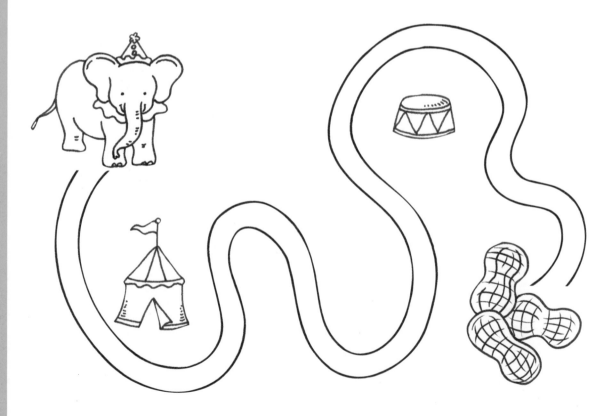

Fill in the ◯.

1. Find the capital letter.

   ◯ E

   ◯ e

2. Find the lowercase letter.

   ◯ e

   ◯ E

3. Find the elephant.

  ◯   ◯

Give the spelling test. Say:

1. Write a capital E in the box.
2. Write a lowercase e in the box.

Spelling Test

1. ☐

2. ☐

Ff

Fish

Fish

See the fish.

Big and Little

Draw a line to make a match.

See the capital **F**.

See the lowercase **f**.

I Can Write

Trace and write the letters.

F	F	F
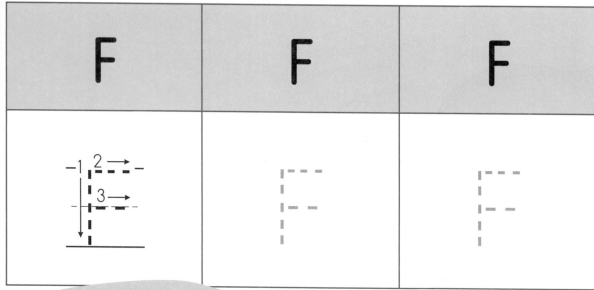		

f	f	f

Spell & Write • EMC 4535 • © Evan-Moor Corp.

Find It

Circle the letters that are the same as the first letter in each row.

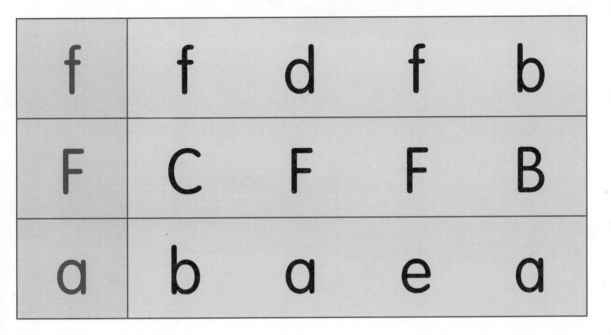

f	f	d	f	b
F	C	F	F	B
a	b	a	e	a

Trace the fishbowl.
Draw an orange fish in the bowl.

Fill in the ○.

1. Find the capital letter.

○ F

○ f

2. Find the lowercase letter.

○ f

○ F

3. Find the fish.

 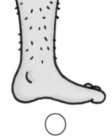

○   ○

Give the spelling test. Say:

1. Write a capital F in the box.

2. Write a lowercase f in the box.

Spelling Test

1.

2.

Gg

Gorilla

Gorilla

See the gorilla.

Big and Little

Draw a line to make a match.

See the capital **G**.

See the lowercase **g**.

UNIT 7

Spell & Write • EMC 4535 • © Evan-Moor Corp.

I Can Write

Trace and write the letters.

G	G	G

g	g	g

Find It

Circle the letters that are the same as the first letter in each row.

g	g	G	b	g
G	G	B	G	C
d	g	d	d	g

Trace the gorilla.
Color him brown.

Fill in the ◯.

1. Find the capital letter.

◯ G

◯ g

2. Find the lowercase letter.

◯ g

◯ G

3. Find the gorilla.

◯ ◯

Give the spelling test. Say:

1. Write a capital G in the box.
2. Write a lowercase g in the box.

Spelling Test

1.

2.

Hh

Hen

Hen

See the hen.

Big and Little

Draw a line to make a match.

See the capital **H**.

See the lowercase **h**.

I Can Write

Trace and write the letters.

H	H	H

h	h	h

Find It

Circle the letters that are the same as the first letter in each row.

H	h	H	G	H
h	b	h	h	d
g	a	g	b	g

Finish drawing the hen.
Make both sides the same.

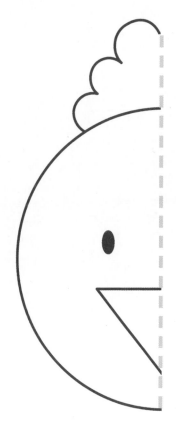

Fill in the ○.

1. Find the capital letter.

   ○ H

   ○ h

2. Find the lowercase letter.

   ○ h

   ○ H

3. Find the hen.

○   ○

Give the spelling test. Say:

1. Write a capital H in the box.
2. Write a lowercase h in the box.

Spelling Test

1. ☐

2. ☐

I i

Ice cream
Ice cream
See the ice cream.

Skills:

Matching
Upper- and
Lowercase
Forms of
Letters

Using Visual
Discrimination

Big and Little

Draw a line to make a match.

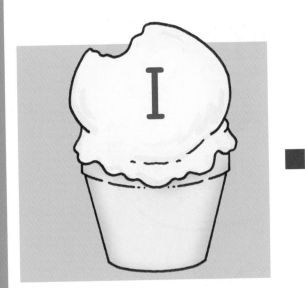

See the capital **I**.

See the lowercase **i**.

(44) UNIT 9

I Can Write

Trace and write the letters.

I	I	I

i	i	i

Find It

Circle the letters that are the same as the first letter in each row.

I	I	i	H	I
i	l	i	i	h
H	H	B	H	A

Finish drawing the ice-cream cone.
Color it.

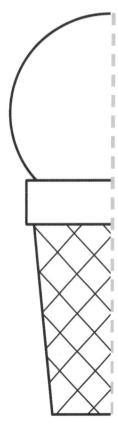

Fill in the ◯.

1. Find the capital letter.

◯ I

◯ i

2. Find the lowercase letter.

◯ i

◯ I

3. Find the ice-cream cone.

◯   ◯

Give the spelling test. Say:

1. Write a capital I in the box.

2. Write a lowercase i in the box.

Spelling Test

1.

2.

ASSESSMENT 9   **47**

J j

Jelly

Jelly

See the jellyfish.

Note: Throughout the book, read and explain all directions to your child. Provide any needed help to complete the tasks.

Big and Little

Skills:

Matching Upper- and Lowercase Forms of Letters

Using Visual Discrimination

Draw a line to make a match.

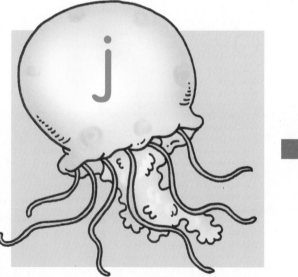

See the capital **J**.

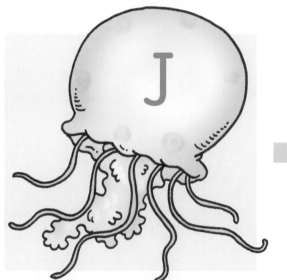

See the lowercase j.

I Can Write

Trace and write the letters.

J	J	J

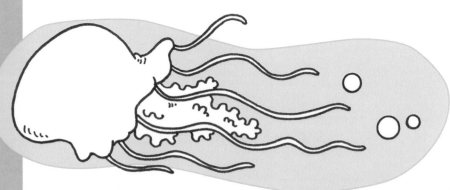

j	j	j

Find It

Circle the letters that are the same as the first letter in each row.

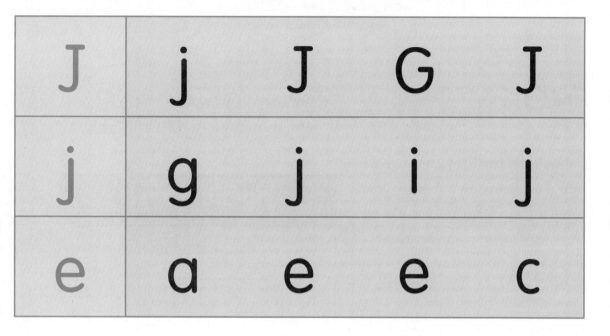

J	j	J	G	J
j	g	j	i	j
e	a	e	e	c

Trace the jellyfish.
Color it blue.

TEST YOUR SKILLS

Fill in the ○.

1. Find the capital letter.

○ J

○ j

2. Find the lowercase letter.

○ j

○ J

3. Find the jellyfish.

○   ○

Give the spelling test. Say:

1. Write a capital J in the box.

2. Write a lowercase j in the box.

Spelling Test

1. ⬜

2. ⬜

K k

Kangaroo
Kangaroo
See the kangaroo.

Skills:

Matching Upper- and Lowercase Forms of Letters

Using Visual Discrimination

Big and Little

Draw a line to make a match.

See the capital **K**.

See the lowercase **k**.

I Can Write

Trace and write the letters.

K	K	K
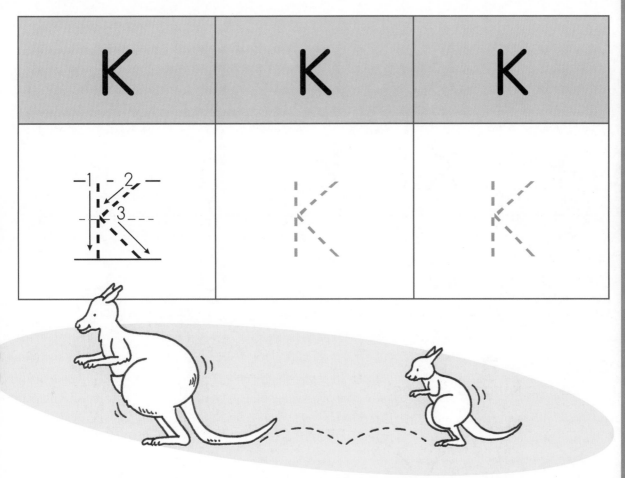	K	K

k	k	k
k	k	k

Find It

Circle the letters that are the same as the first letter in each row.

K	k	h	K	K
k	K	k	h	k
g	b	g	g	d

Start at the ★.
Trace the kangaroo's hops.

Fill in the ○.

1. Find the capital letter.

○ K

○ k

2. Find the lowercase letter.

○ k

○ K

3. Find the kangaroo.

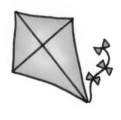 

○   ○

Give the spelling test. Say:
1. Write a capital K in the box.
2. Write a lowercase k in the box.

Spelling Test

1. ▢

2. ▢

ASSESSMENT 11   **57**

L l

Lambs
Lambs
See the lambs.

Note: Throughout the book, read and explain all directions to your child. Provide any needed help to complete the tasks.

Big and Little

Draw a line to make a match.

See the capital L.

See the lowercase l.

I Can Write

Trace and write the letters.

L	L	L

I	I	I

Find It

Circle the letters that are the same as the first letter in each row.

L	G	L	H	L
l	l	h	b	l
j	g	j	J	j

Trace the lamb.
Color it.

TEST YOUR SKILLS

Fill in the ◯.

1. Find the capital letter.

◯ L

◯ l

2. Find the lowercase letter.

◯ l

◯ L

3. Find the lamb.

◯   ◯

Give the spelling test. Say:
1. Write a capital L in the box.
2. Write a lowercase l in the box.

Spelling Test

1. ☐

2. ☐

Mm

Mouse

Mouse

See the mouse.

Big and Little

Draw a line to make a match.

See the capital **M**.

See the lowercase **m**.

I Can Write

Trace and write the letters.

M	M	M

m	m	m

Find It

Circle the letters that are the same as the first letter in each row.

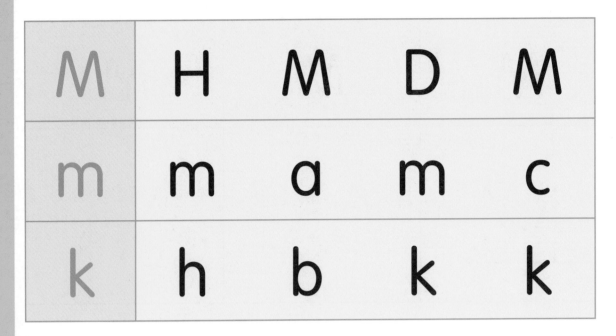

M	H	M	D	M
m	m	a	m	c
k	h	b	k	k

Trace the path to the cheese.
Color the mouse gray. Color the cheese orange.

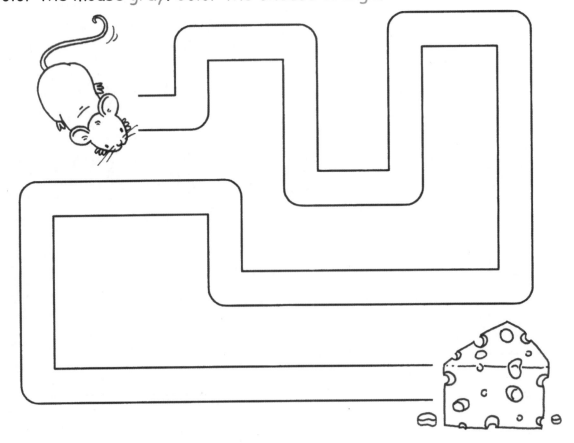

Fill in the ○.

1. Find the capital letter.

   ○ **M**

   ○ **m**

2. Find the lowercase letter.

   ○ **m**

   ○ **M**

3. Find the mouse.

Give the spelling test. Say:
1. Write a capital M in the box.
2. Write a lowercase m in the box.

Spelling Test

1. ☐

2. ☐

Nn

Nest

Nest

See the nest.

Note: Throughout the book, read and explain all directions to your child. Provide any needed help to complete the tasks.

Big and Little

Draw a line to make a match.

Skills:

Matching Upper- and Lowercase Forms of Letters

Using Visual Discrimination

See the capital **N**.

.

See the lowercase **n**.

.

I Can Write

Trace and write the letters.

N	N	N

n	n	n

Find It

Circle the letters that are the same as the first letter in each row.

N	N	P	N	M
n	c	n	d	n
c	a	c	c	e

Draw 3 blue eggs in the nest.

TEST YOUR SKILLS

Fill in the ○.

1. Find the capital letter.

○ N

○ n

2. Find the lowercase letter.

○ n

○ N

3. Find the nest.

○   ○

Give the spelling test. Say:

1. Write a capital N in the box.
2. Write a lowercase n in the box.

Spelling Test

1. ☐

2. ☐

Oo

Octopus

Octopus

See the octopus.

Big and Little

Draw a line to make a match.

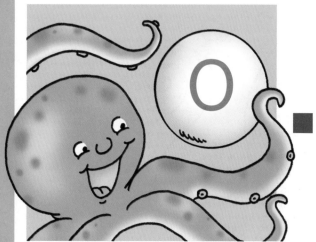

See the capital **O**.

See the lowercase **o**.

I Can Write

Trace and write the letters.

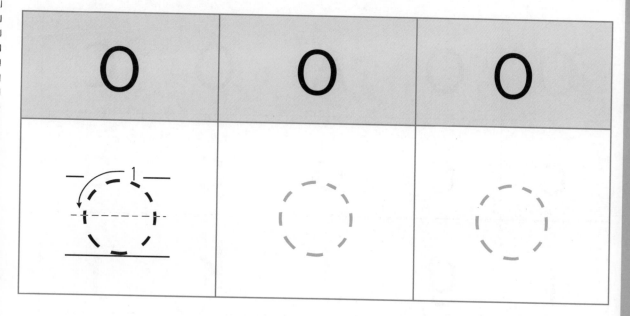

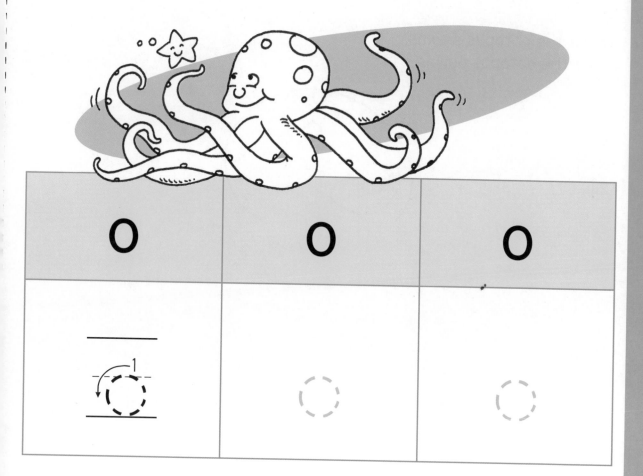

Find It

Skills:

Identifying Like Letters

Using Fine Motor Skills

Circle the letters that are the same as the first letter in each row.

O	O	A	O	C
c	c	o	c	a
j	g	j	k	j

Trace the octopus's arms.
Color the octopus purple.

Spell & Write • EMC 4535 • © Evan-Moor Corp.

Fill in the ◯.

1. Find the capital letter.

◯ O

◯ o

2. Find the lowercase letter.

◯ o

◯ O

3. Find the octopus.

◯ ◯

Give the spelling test. Say:

1. Write a capital O in the box.
2. Write a lowercase o in the box.

Spelling Test

1. ▢

2. ▢

P p

Pigs

Pigs

See the pigs.

Big and Little

Draw a line to make a match.

Skills:

Matching Upper- and Lowercase Forms of Letters

Using Visual Discrimination

See the capital **P**.

See the lowercase **p**.

I Can Write

Trace and write the letters.

P	P	P

p	p	p

Find It

Circle the letters that are the same as the first letter in each row.

P	P	D	M	P
p	g	j	p	p
m	m	o	m	e

Trace the pig.
Color the pig's spots brown.

TEST YOUR SKILLS

Fill in the ◯.

1. Find the capital letter.

◯ P

◯ p

2. Find the lowercase letter.

◯ p

◯ P

3. Find the pig.

◯   ◯

Give the spelling test. Say:

1. Write a capital P in the box.

2. Write a lowercase p in the box.

Spelling Test

1. ☐

2. ☐

Qq

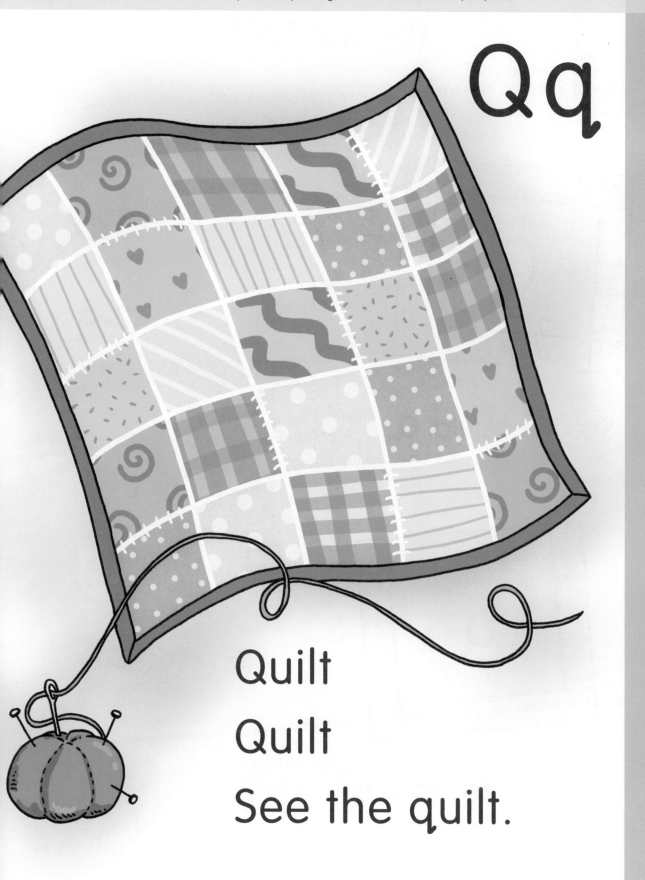

Quilt

Quilt

See the quilt.

Big and Little

Draw a line to make a match.

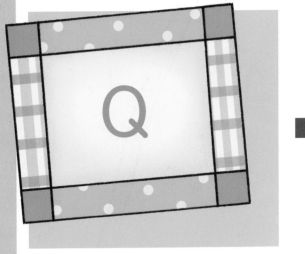

See the capital **Q**.

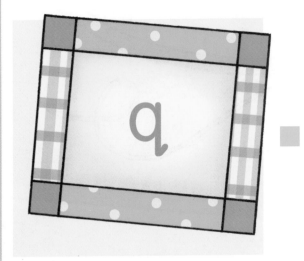

See the lowercase **q**.

I Can Write

Trace and write the letters.

Q	Q	Q

q	q	q

Skills:

Identifying Like Letters

Using Fine Motor Skills

Find It

Circle the letters that are the same as the first letter in each row.

Q	P	Q	Q	O
q	q	g	q	d
G	O	G	Q	G

Color the quilt.
Color the heart red.

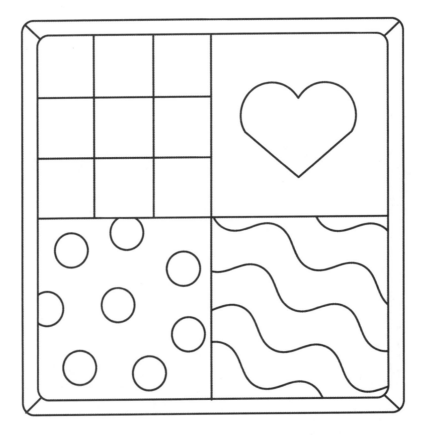

Fill in the ◯.

1. Find the capital letter.

   ◯ **Q**

   ◯ **q**

2. Find the lowercase letter.

   ◯ **q**

   ◯ **Q**

3. Find the quilt.

Give the spelling test. Say:

1. Write a capital **Q** in the box.
2. Write a lowercase **q** in the box.

Spelling Test

1.

2.

Rr

Rabbit

Rabbit

See the rabbit.

Big and Little

Draw a line to make a match.

See the capital **R**.

See the lowercase **r**.

I Can Write

Trace and write the letters.

R	R	R
	R	R

r	r	r
	r	r

Spell & Write • EMC 4535 • © Evan-Moor Corp.

Find It

Circle the letters that are the same as the first letter in each row.

r	r	c	r	n
R	P	R	R	G
B	B	D	G	B

Finish coloring the carrot.
Make both sides match.

TEST YOUR SKILLS

Fill in the ⬭ .

1. Find the capital letter.

○ R

○ r

2. Find the lowercase letter.

○ r

○ R

3. Find the rabbit.

○

Give the spelling test. Say:
1. Write a capital R in the box.
2. Write a lowercase r in the box.

Spelling Test

1. ☐

2. ☐

S s

Sun

Sun

See the sun.

Skills:

Matching
Upper- and
Lowercase
Forms of
Letters

Using Visual
Discrimination

Big and Little

Draw a line to make a match.

See the capital **S**.

See the lowercase **s**.

I Can Write

Trace and write the letters.

S	S	S
S	S	S

S	S	S
S	S	S

Find It

Circle the letters that are the same as the first letter in each row.

S	R	C	S	S
s	r	s	m	s
q	q	j	h	q

Trace the sun.
Color it yellow.

TEST YOUR SKILLS

Fill in the ○.

1. Find the capital letter.

○ S

○ s

2. Find the lowercase letter.

○ s

○ S

3. Find the sun.

○   ○

Give the spelling test. Say:

1. Write a capital S in the box.
2. Write a lowercase S in the box.

Spelling Test

1. ☐

2. ☐

T t

Turtle

Turtle

See the turtle.

Big and Little

Draw a line to make a match.

Skills:

Matching Upper- and Lowercase Forms of Letters

Using Visual Discrimination

See the capital **T**.

See the lowercase **t**.

I Can Write

Trace and write the letters.

T	T	T
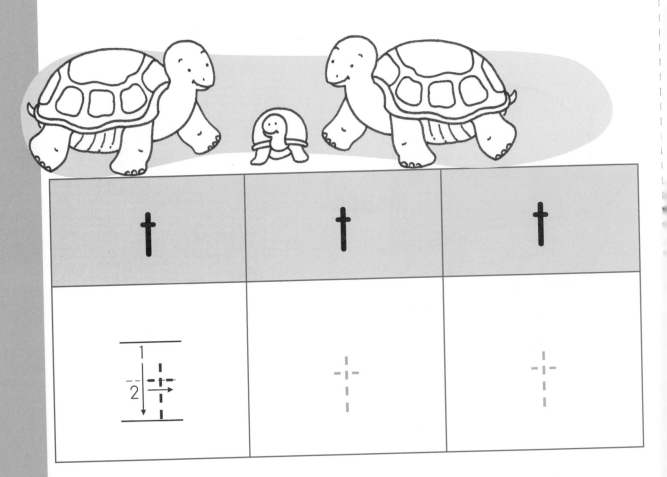		

†	†	†

Find It

Circle the letters that are the same as the first letter in each row.

T	T	H	T	L
t	h	i	t	t
L	L	L	T	I

Trace the turtle's shell.
Color it green.

Fill in the ○ .

1. Find the capital letter.

○ T

○ t

2. Find the lowercase letter.

○ t

○ T

3. Find the turtle.

○

Give the spelling test. Say:
1. Write a capital T in the box.
2. Write a lowercase t in the box.

Spelling Test

1.

2.

Uu

Umbrella

Umbrella

See the umbrella.

Big and Little

Draw a line to make a match.

See the capital **U**.

See the lowercase **u**.

I Can Write

Trace and write the letters.

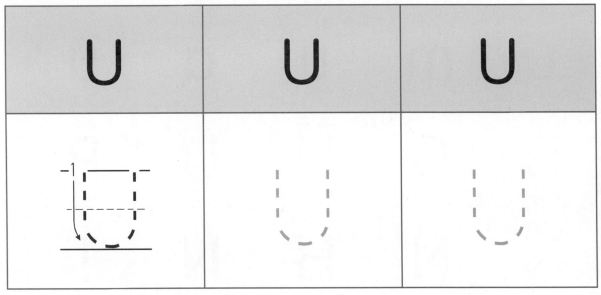

Find It

Circle the letters that are the same as the first letter in each row.

u	m	u	a	u
U	O	U	U	P
N	N	H	N	T

Trace the umbrella.
Color it purple.

Spell & Write • EMC 4535 • © Evan-Moor Corp.

TEST YOUR SKILLS

Fill in the ○.

1. Find the capital letter.

○ U

○ u

2. Find the lowercase letter.

○ u

○ U

3. Find the umbrella.

○   ○

Give the spelling test. Say:
1. Write a capital U in the box.
2. Write a lowercase u in the box.

Spelling Test

1. ☐

2. ☐

V v

Vest

Vest

See the vest.

Big and Little

Draw a line to make a match.

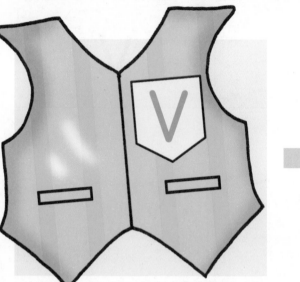

See the capital **V**.

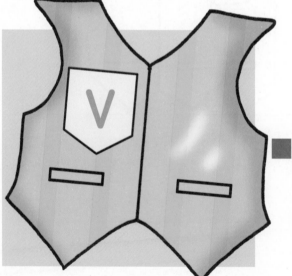

See the lowercase **v**.

I Can Write

Trace and write the letters.

V	V	V

V	V	V

Find It

Circle the letters that are the same as the first letter in each row.

V	N	V	A	V
v	v	u	v	r
m	n	m	m	u

Trace the vest.
Color it.

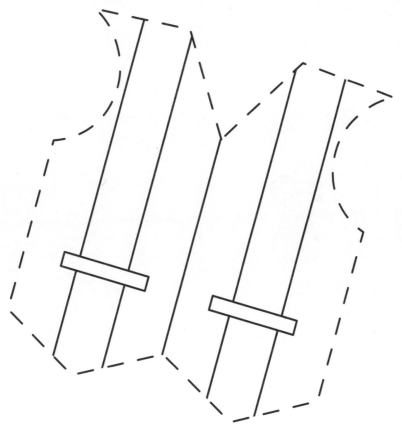

TEST YOUR SKILLS

Fill in the ○.

1. Find the capital letter.

    ○   V

    ○   v

2. Find the lowercase letter.

    ○   v

    ○   V

3. Find the vest.

   ○   ○

Give the spelling test. Say:

1. Write a capital V in the box.
2. Write a lowercase V in the box.

Spelling Test

1.

2.

Ww

Wagon

Wagon

See the wagon.

Skills:

Matching
Upper- and
Lowercase
Forms of
Letters

Using Visual
Discrimination

Big and Little

Draw a line to make a match.

See the capital **W**.

See the lowercase **w**.

114 UNIT 23

I Can Write

Trace and write the letters.

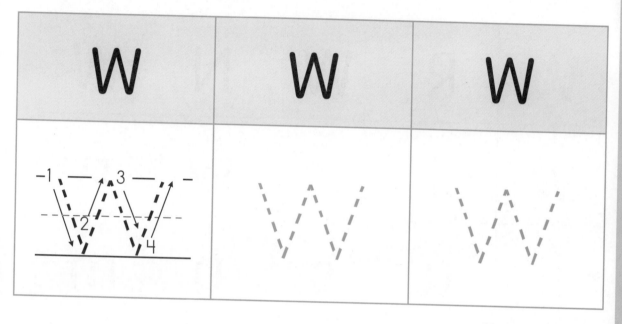

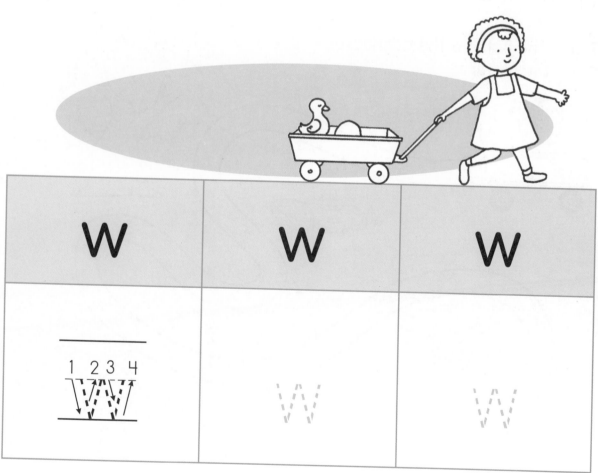

Skills:

Identifying Like Letters

Using Fine Motor Skills

Circle the letters that are the same as the first letter in each row.

W	R	W	N	W
w	s	w	w	n
u	u	s	u	m

Trace the path to the doghouse.
Color the picture.

TEST YOUR SKILLS

Fill in the ○.

1. Find the capital letter.

○ W

○ w

2. Find the lowercase letter.

○ w

○ W

3. Find the wagon with the dog in it.

○   ○

Give the spelling test. Say:
1. Write a capital W in the box.
2. Write a lowercase w in the box.

Spelling Test

1. ☐

2. ☐

X x

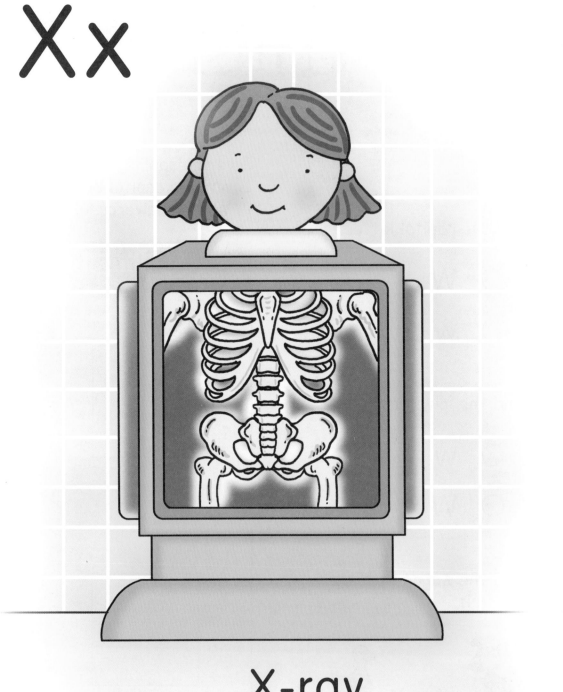

X-ray

X-ray

See the X-ray.

Note: Throughout the book, read and explain all directions to your child. Provide any needed help to complete the tasks.

Big and Little

Draw a line to make a match.

See the capital **X**.

See the lowercase **X**.

I Can Write

Trace and write the letters.

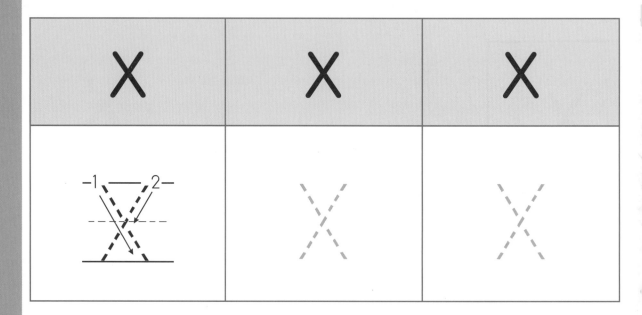

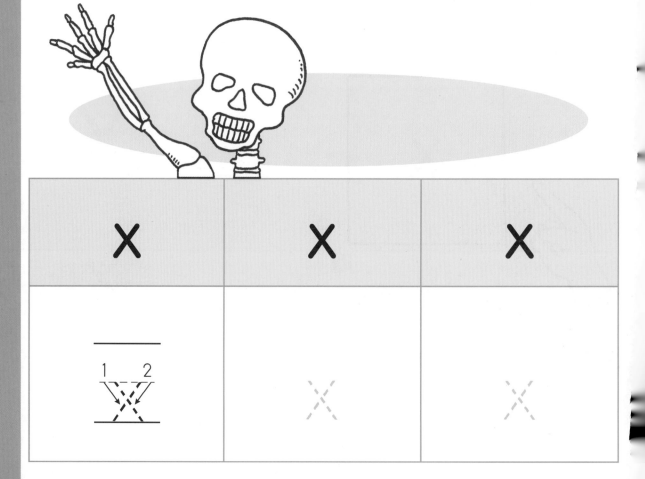

Spell & Write • EMC 4535 • © Evan-Moor Corp.

Find It

Circle the letters that are the same as the first letter in each row.

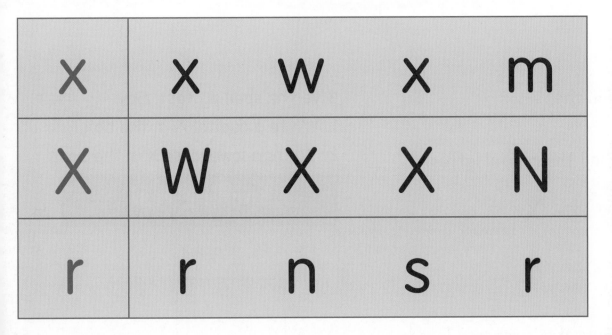

x	x	w	x	m
X	W	X	X	N
r	r	n	s	r

Find the bones.
Color them.

Fill in the ⭕.

1. Find the capital letter.

⭕ X

⭕ x

2. Find the lowercase letter.

⭕ x

⭕ X

3. Find the X-ray of a hand.

⭕   ⭕

Give the spelling test. Say:

1. Write a capital X in the box.

2. Write a lowercase X in the box.

Spelling Test

1. ⬜

2. ⬜

Y y

Yarn

Yarn

See the yarn.

Big and Little

Draw a line to make a match.

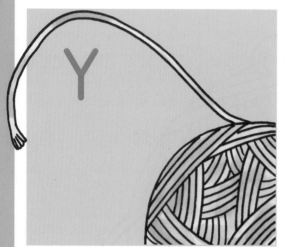

See the capital **Y**.

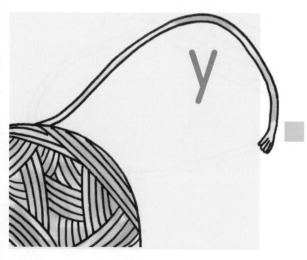

See the lowercase **y**.

I Can Write

Trace and write the letters.

Y	Y	Y
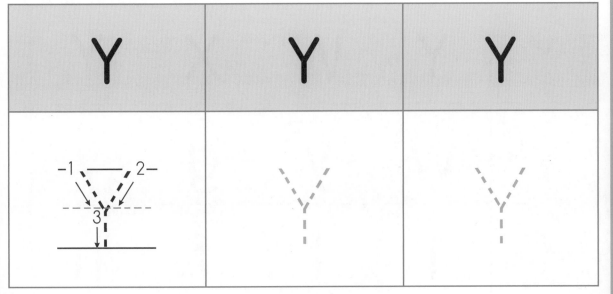		

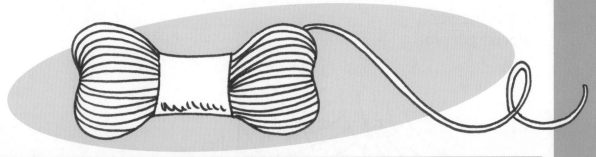

y	y	y

Find It

Circle the letters that are the same as the first letter in each row.

Y	Y	W	X	Y
y	w	y	g	y
f	t	f	f	h

Trace the yarn.
Color it purple.

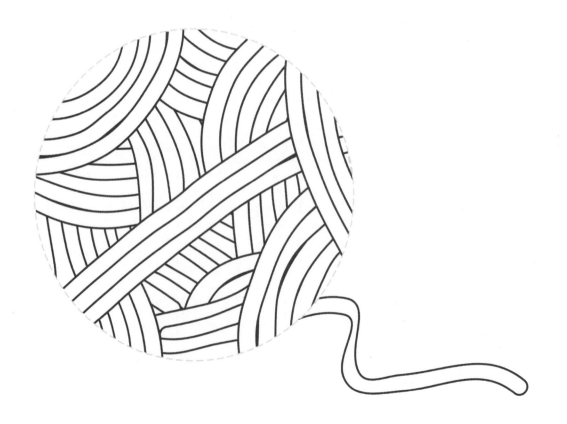

TEST YOUR SKILLS

Fill in the ○.

1. Find the capital letter.

○ Y

○ y

2. Find the lowercase letter.

○ Y

○ y

3. Find the yellow yarn.

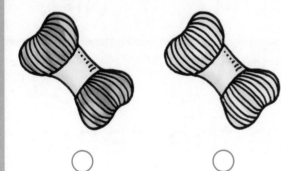

○   ○

Give the spelling test. Say:

1. Write a capital Y in the box.

2. Write a lowercase y in the box.

Spelling Test

1. ☐

2. ☐

Zz

Zebra

Zebra

See the zebra.

Note: Throughout the book, read and explain all directions to your child. Provide any needed help to complete the tasks.

Big and Little

Draw a line to make a match.

See the capital **Z**.

See the lowercase **z**.

I Can Write

Trace and write the letters.

Z	Z	Z
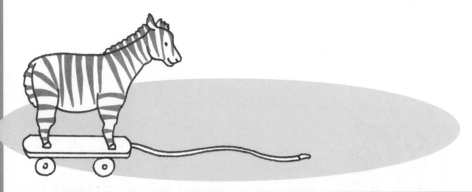		

Z	Z	Z

Find It

Circle the letters that are the same as the first letter in each row.

Z	Z	X	W	Z
Z	X	Z	V	Z
W	X	W	Z	W

Trace the path.
Help the zebra find his friend.

Fill in the ○.

1. Find the capital letter.

○ Z

○ z

2. Find the lowercase letter.

○ z

○ Z

3. Find the zebra.

 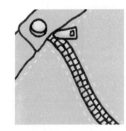

○ ○

Give the spelling test. Say:
1. Write a capital Z in the box.
2. Write a lowercase z in the box.

Spelling Test

1.

2.

Test Your Skills—Record Form

Unit	Test Page	Topic	Test Your Skills Score (3 possible)	Spelling Test Score (2 possible)
1	7	**Aa** alligator		
2	12	**Bb** baby		
3	17	**Cc** cat		
4	22	**Dd** dinosaur		
5	27	**Ee** elephant		
6	32	**Ff** fish		
7	37	**Gg** gorilla		
8	42	**Hh** hen		
9	47	**Ii** ice cream		
10	52	**Jj** jellyfish		
11	57	**Kk** kangaroo		
12	62	**Ll** lamb		
13	67	**Mm** mouse		

Test Your Skills—Record Form

Unit	Test Page	Topic	Test Your Skills Score (3 possible)	Spelling Test Score (2 possible)
14	72	**Nn** nest		
15	77	**Oo** octopus		
16	82	**Pp** pig		
17	87	**Qq** quilt		
18	92	**Rr** rabbit		
19	97	**Ss** sun		
20	102	**Tt** turtle		
21	107	**Uu** umbrella		
22	112	**Vv** vest		
23	117	**Ww** wagon		
24	122	**Xx** X-ray		
25	127	**Yy** yarn		
26	132	**Zz** zebra		

Spell & Write • EMC 4535 • © Evan-Moor Corp.

Answer Key

Page 4

Page 6

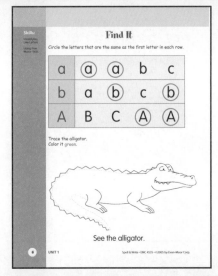

Page 7

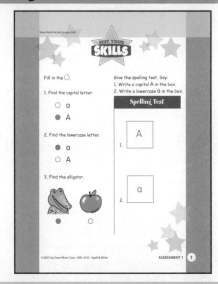

Page 9

Page 11

Page 12

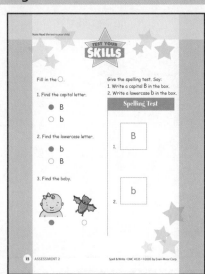

Page 14

Page 16

Page 17

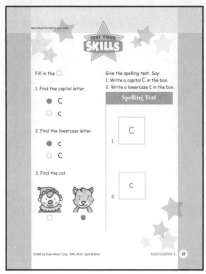

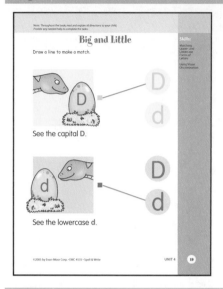

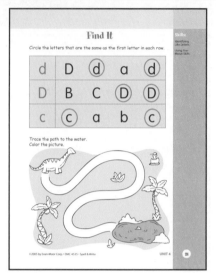

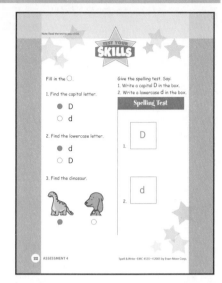

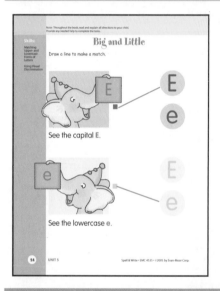

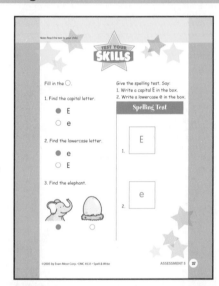

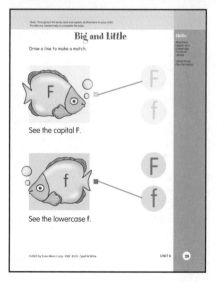

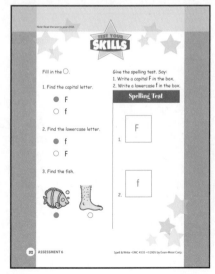

Spell & Write • EMC 4535 • © Evan-Moor Corp.

Page 34

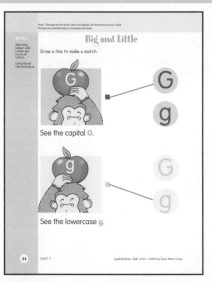

Page 36

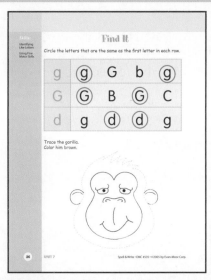

Page 37

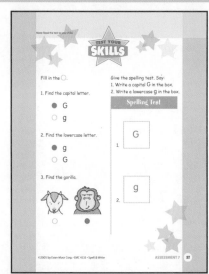

Page 39

Page 41

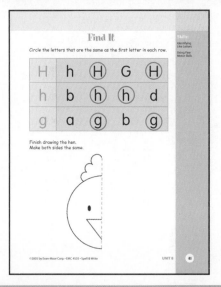

Page 42

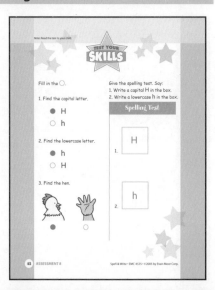

Page 44

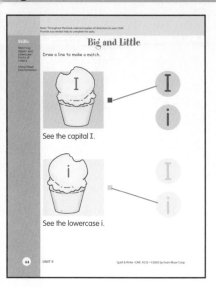

Page 46

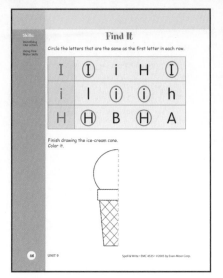

Page 47

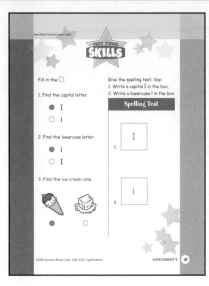

Page 49

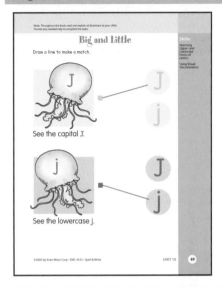

Page 51

Page 52

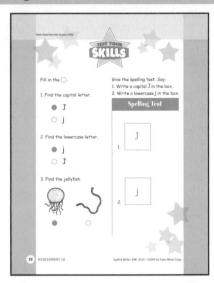

Page 54

Page 56

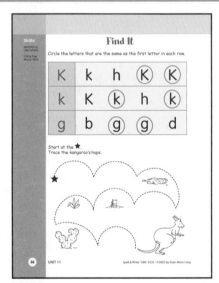

Page 57

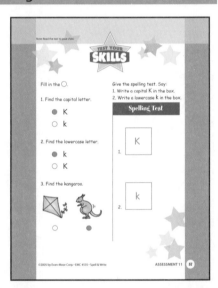

Page 59

Page 61

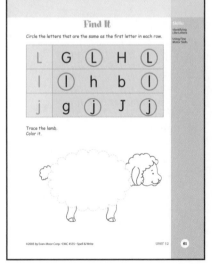

Page 62

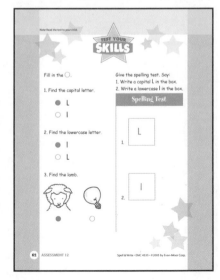

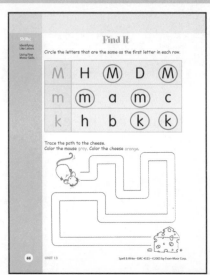

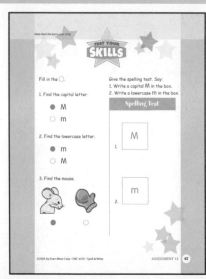

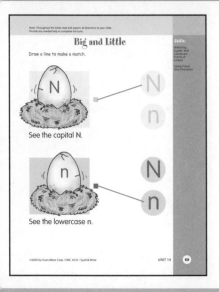

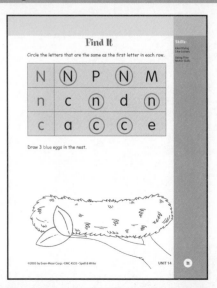

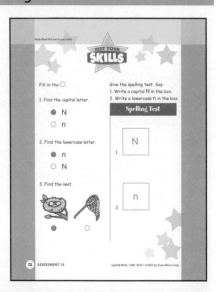

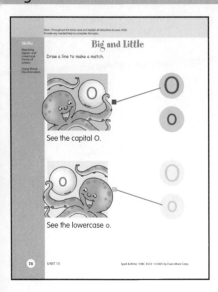

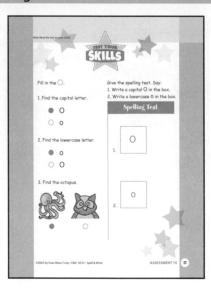

Page 79

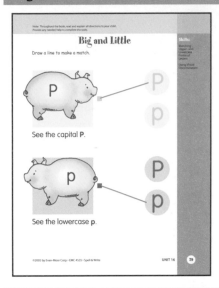

Page 81

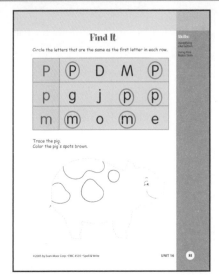

Page 82

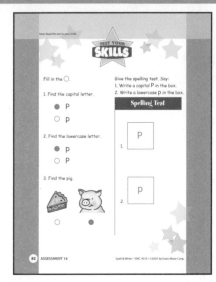

Page 84

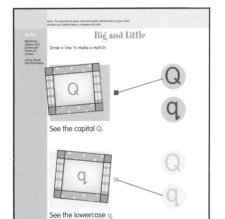

Page 86

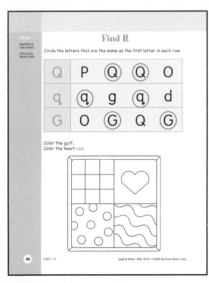

Page 87

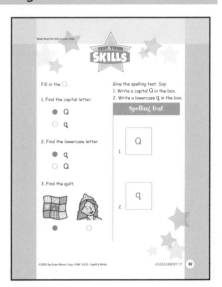

Page 89

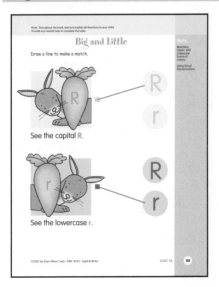

Page 91

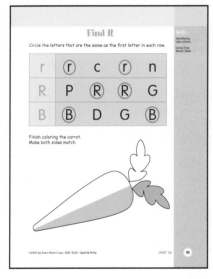

Page 92

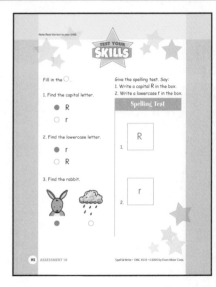

Spell & Write • EMC 4535 • © Evan-Moor Corp.

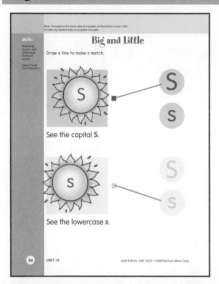

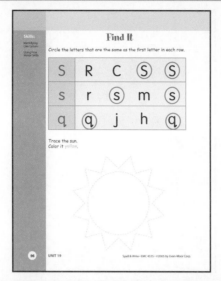

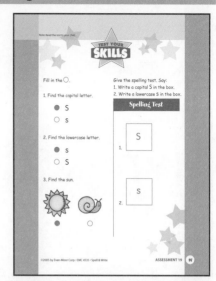

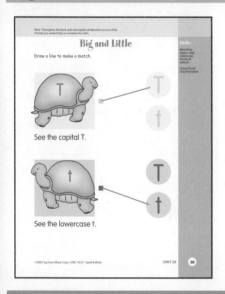

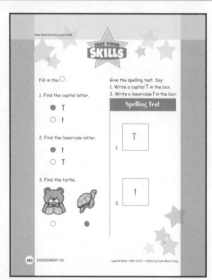

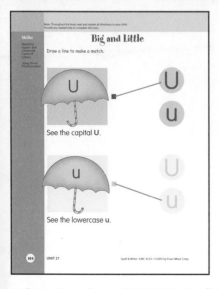

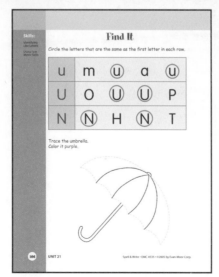

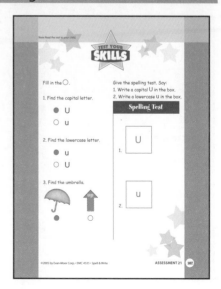

Page 109

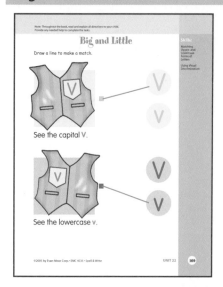

Page 111

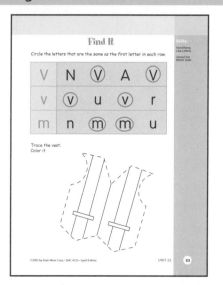

Page 112

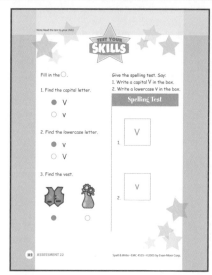

Page 114

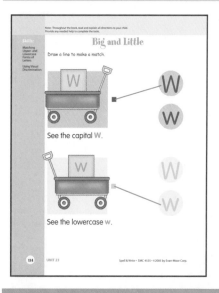

Page 116

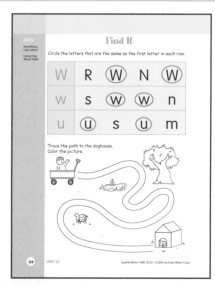

Page 117

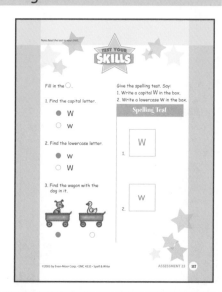

Page 119

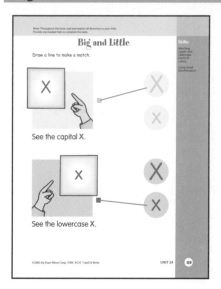

Page 121

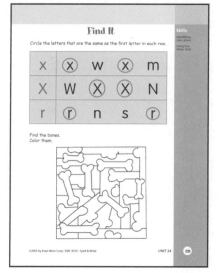

Page 122

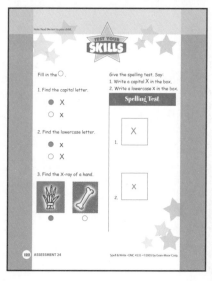

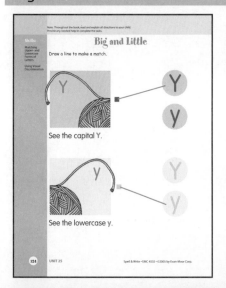

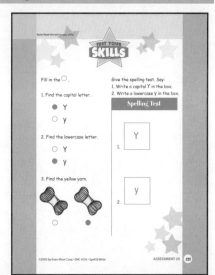

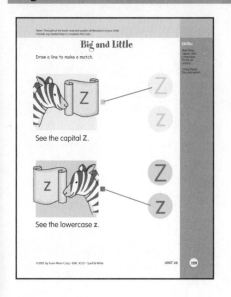

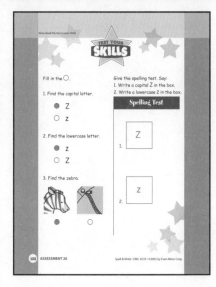